The Ultimate Guide to HOA Painting:

What Every Board Member and Property Manager Should Know

From the publishers:

Pacific Western Painting, Inc. (PWP) and its expert painters can meet the painting needs of any community, but whether or not they're given the opportunity it's their mission to deliver the best information into the hands of HOA decision-makers. *The Ultimate Guide to HOA Painting* is an all-inclusive research tool designed to navigate the process of finding the best contractor step by step, from vetting to project completion. Essential before the hunt for a painting contractor begins, this HOA resource not only takes the guesswork out of the search, but it's also a sure way to avoid unnecessary stress, procrastination and costly mistakes, and guarantee a successful project.

Contents

Contents
Introduction
To Paint or
Not to Paint?
Brush Up on
Painting Basics:
What HOAs
Can Expect
More Area
to Cover
Glossary

Introduction

To Paint or Not to Paint?

Brush up on Painting Basics: What HOAs Can Expect

More Area to Cover

Glossary

Introduction
Painting Maintenance Profits HOAs

From coast to coast, painting maintenance has claimed a permanent spot atop the home industry's "Best Ways to Increase Property Value" lists. For years, real estate experts have endorsed repainting and exterior upgrading as smart investments, and savvy homeowners who follow their advice continue to reap the rewards of getting the most for their money. Over the past four decades, many of those owners have also been influenced by another industry trend that shows no signs of slowing: Homeowner's Associations (HOAs).

Comprised of property owners in a common-interest development, U.S. HOAs totaled less than 10,000 in 1970, but the latest statistics reveal that over 40 million households are now governed by HOAs. In just California, there are currently 35,000 - 40,000 community associations comprising 3 million units -- condominiums, townhomes and single family homes -- totaling about 450 billion dollars in property values, with more being built daily.

U.S. HOAs totaled less than 10,000 in 1970, but the latest statistics reveal that over 40 million households are now governed by HOAs.

HOA fees pay for amenities such as landscaping, heated pools, tennis courts, clubhouses, property management, security and much more. Regular home maintenance and well-kept neighborhoods mean stable property value, which make common-interest real estate attractive to buyers.

Before:

After:

On Board to Choose Wisely

Every HOA elects a board of directors consisting of owners in the association to manage all community matters. Among the board's duties performed on the association's behalf is the contracting of common area goods and services that include the formidable task of choosing a painting provider. With countless contractors to choose from, board members have a lot riding on selecting the best one for their particular improvement needs. HOA painting and its timely upkeep are considerable expenditures, and no board wants to make mistakes that negatively impact its community's property value and budget. After all, its goal is to protect the equity that owners have established in their homes, which for many are their largest assets.

Managed and maintained properly, painting can last for many years. Neglected or postponed for too long, it may survive less than half that time – especially on structures near the beach that need extra maintenance. More often than not, however, HOA board members possess little painting knowledge, and the duties of identifying, comparing and choosing a reputable, professional company can lead to frustration, further delay or shelving projects indefinitely. Meanwhile, exposure to the elements wreak havoc on coated surfaces and the longer repairs are put off, the more complicated decisions board members face. The results: additional cost and inconvenience for residents.

The Answers at a Glance

Though an HOA's property manager is usually the one accountable for handling construction-related issues, board members should have at least some idea of what they're looking for in a painting provider. The founders of Pacific Western Painting (PWP), Inc., committed to better serving HOAs and improving the quality of contractors, recognize that a successful painting job begins with knowing what maintenance is needed and how to proceed. To that end, they've compiled everything board members and property managers need to know into this guide -- from quotes to completion and beyond.

Designed specifically for HOA officers without construction backgrounds, *The Ultimate Guide* streamlines all the essentials necessary to make informed, painting-related decisions, preempting many job hiccups and ensuring success. Organized in user-friendly, accessible sections that make finding specific data a cinch, this comprehensive resource also contains charts, checklists, photos and a glossary to help with unfamiliar terms.

HOA Painting: Covering the Surfaces

HOA painting may include coating the following substrates:

Wood Substrates

- address letters/numbers
- benches
- bridges
- carport cabinets
- carport poles and structures
- corbels
- decking
- door frames and jambs
- entry doors
- fascias
- fencing
- French doors
- garage doors and frames
- gates
- gazebos
- hardboard siding
- louvers
- mailbox structures and posts
- map kiosks
- monument signs
- panels
- patio covers
- planter boxes and shelves
- plant ons
- plywood siding T-111
- pool shade structures
- rafter tails
- railings
- shingle siding
- shutters
- soffits
- stair risers
- stringers and treads
- street signage
- support poles
- trash enclosures
- trellises
- vents
- window frames and trim

Metal Substrates

- air-conditioning units
- awnings
- balcony rails
- cable wire housing
- ceiling-mount light fixtures
- chain-link fencing
- chimney caps
- closet doors
- downspouts
- entry kiosks
- fire extinguisher boxes
- flag poles
- flashing
- garage doors
- gas meters
- gates
- gutters
- light poles
- louvers
- mansard (French) roofs
- ornamental wrought iron
- panels
- piping
- conduit wiring
- roof access ladders and jacks
- scuppers
- security bars and screen doors
- spark arrestors
- stair railings
- steel pipe railings
- trash enclosure gate frames
- utility box covers
- utility doors
- vents
- wall mount light fixtures
- water spigots
- window frames
- wrought iron

Masonry Substrates

- beams
- bollards
- clubhouses
- columns
- concrete brick/
  CMU block
- curbing
- eaves
- entry doors
- fascias
- fences
- foundations
- freestanding common
  area walls
- light pole bases
- monument signs
- overhangs
- parapet walls
- parking area striping
- parking garage walls
  and ceilings
- patio and perimeter
  walls
- planters
- pony walls
- pool fences
- recreational courts
- retaining walls
- siding
- soffits
- stairs
- storage units
- stucco
- trash enclosure walls
- trim

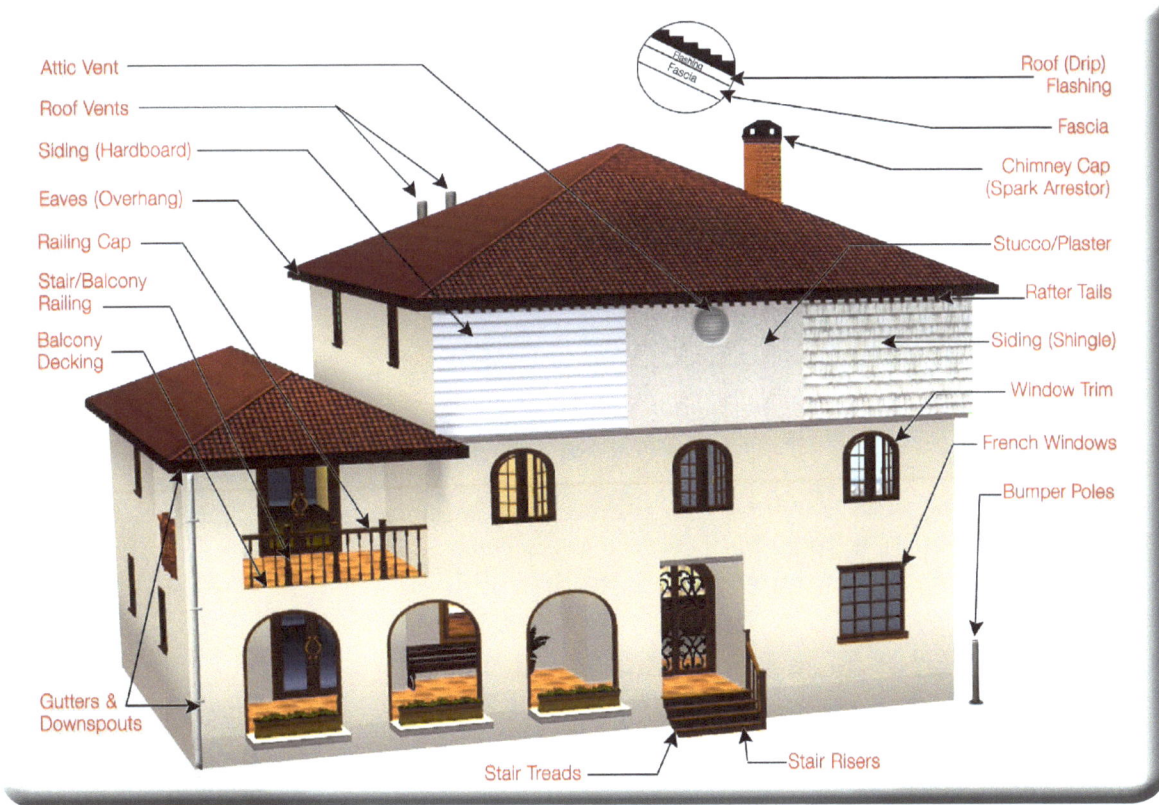

Attic Vent
Roof Vents
Siding (Hardboard)
Eaves (Overhang)
Railing Cap
Stair/Balcony Railing
Balcony Decking
Gutters & Downspouts
Stair Treads
Stair Risers
Flashing Fascia
Roof (Drip) Flashing
Fascia
Chimney Cap (Spark Arrestor)
Stucco/Plaster
Rafter Tails
Siding (Shingle)
Window Trim
French Windows
Bumper Poles

To Paint Or Not To Paint?

Paint has a lifecycle. It starts out fresh and clean, then ages, weathers and eventually deteriorates. Paint's longevity is affected by several factors, including the application, environment, products, preparation, frequency of inspections and the surfaces, or substrates, being painted.

Stages of Painting Maintenance

Typically, HOA painting maintenance includes the following stages:

Stage 1: New Paint (0 - 2 years)
- Little or no maintenance required
- Inspection of metal surfaces

Stage 2: Preliminary Preventive Maintenance (2 - 4 years)
- Spot prime and paint metal (recommended at 2 years)
- Power wash, caulk and patch cracks in masonry and wood

Stage 3: Minor Repairs (4 - 6 years)
- Power wash, patch repair and seal cracks on masonry and wood
- Spot prime and repaint wood (recommended at 3 - 5 years)

Stage 4: Major Repairs (6 - 8 years)
- Power wash, patch repair and seal cracks on masonry and wood
- Paint wood if needed
- Spot prime and repaint masonry (recommended at 7 - 8 years)

Stage 5: Recommended Repaint (8+ years)
- Power wash, restore and repaint all substrates throughout the community

The Life Cycle of Painting

Exterior Masonry Paint

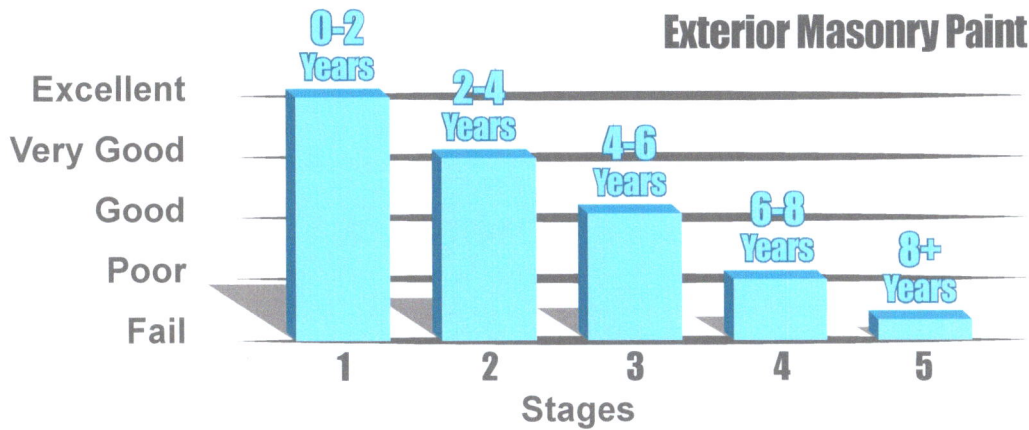

Stages: 1 (0-2 Years), 2 (2-4 Years), 3 (4-6 Years), 4 (6-8 Years), 5 (8+ Years)

Ratings: Excellent, Very Good, Good, Poor, Fail

Exterior Wood Paint

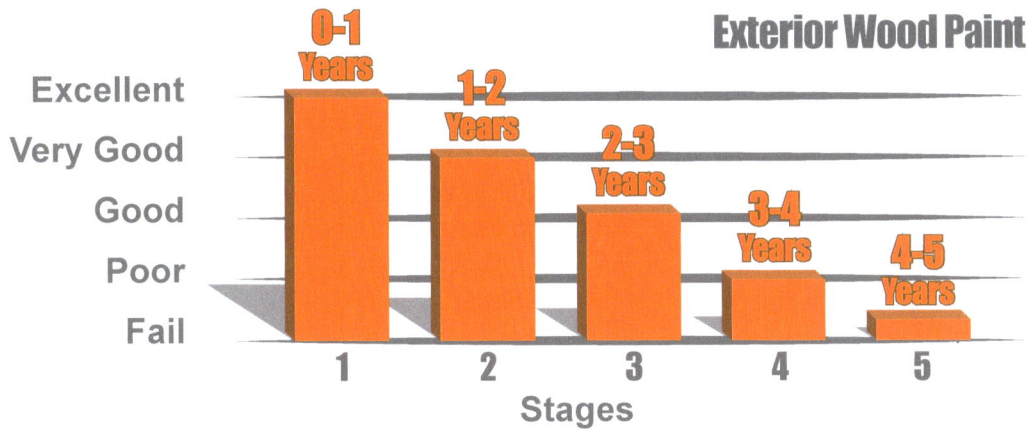

Stages: 1 (0-1 Years), 2 (1-2 Years), 3 (2-3 Years), 4 (3-4 Years), 5 (4-5 Years)

Ratings: Excellent, Very Good, Good, Poor, Fail

Exterior Metal Paint

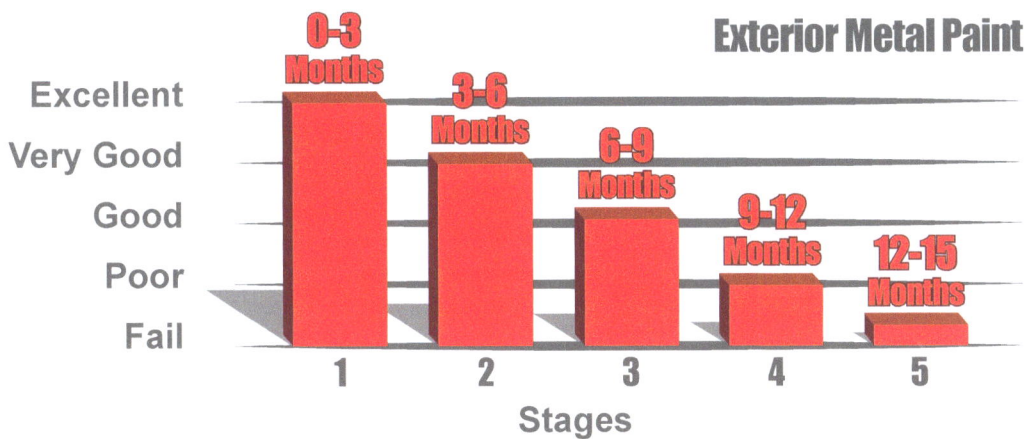

Stages: 1 (0-3 Months), 2 (3-6 Months), 3 (6-9 Months), 4 (9-12 Months), 5 (12-15 Months)

Ratings: Excellent, Very Good, Good, Poor, Fail

The Last Word on Lasting

The following chart shows paint's average lifespan by the surface it's coating.

Surface	Material	Years Will Last
Cement Siding	Exterior Acrylic Paint	7-10
Drywall	Interior Acrylic Paint	7-10
Metal	High Performance Coating	5-7
	Exterior Alkyd Paint	1-2
	Exterior Single Component Urethane	1-2
Stucco	Exterior Acrylic Paint	7-10
Wood	Caulking/Putty	3-5
	Exterior Acrylic Paint	3-5
	Exterior Acrylic Paint on Siding	3-5
	Exterior Oil-Based Paint	2-3
	Interior Oil-Based Paint	3-5
	Lacquer (Interior)	5-10
	Stains	1-2
	Varnishes	1-3

The First Step: Scope of Work

Once a decision to do the work is agreed upon, it's time for the board to pinpoint HOA objectives. With assistance from the property manager or management team, board members will determine and detail in writing exactly what work is needed. This inclusive, written explanation of all project components is called the "scope of work" (SOW).

The purpose of the SOW is to define the spectrum of work needed and duties of both parties, the HOA and painting company. The document will be examined by several people, including potential painting contractors from diverse environments with varying levels of training and experience; therefore, a SOW is prepared carefully to avoid misinterpretation. Wording is straightforward and unambiguous -- not filled with legal-sounding jargon. The more focused the scope of work, the better able contractors will be to construct quotes.

A complete Scope of Work answers the following questions:

- **What is to be done?**
  The activities and milestones necessary to accomplish project objectives.

- **What are the "deliverables?"**
  Deliverables are comprised of required tasks and end products during the course of the job, usually with deadlines.

- **Who is going to do it?**
  A list of all contractors (and subcontractors, if applicable) necessary to accomplish the project plan. Also, person(s) responsible for deliverables.

- **When is it going to be done?**
  Project dates, dates for deliverables, time schedules and relevant deadlines per phase.

- **How will it be done?**
  The specific processes and applications throughout completion.

- **How can you tell when it is done?**
  The manner and standards by which will determine whether tasks and responsibilities are acceptable.

PS: A Supplier's SOW

Another option for HOA boards is to have a paint supplier create a "Paint Specification" (PS), which includes an SOW. Community associations, especially if they prefer a particular paint line, can take advantage of this service that sometimes even incorporates color consultation as incentive for the agreed use of the manufacturer's products.

A PS is a reference tool for both HOA decision-makers, management and contractors that contains detailed information about preparation for specific substrates, application, color, clean up, etc. It also specifies the product line's best performing products for the job, including optimum paint, primer and topcoat gloss levels for all substrates, while taking into consideration lighting, climate exposure and pigment quality. In addition, by committing to a specific paint brand, board members have a standard to evaluate proposals because all contractors bid on those precise products. A PS is also a binding legal document, and should be followed as directed.

XYZ PAINT
12345 E. Sample Address Road
Pier City, CA 32152
Phone: (123) 456-7890
Fax: (123) 456-7891
Mobile: (123) 456-7899
E-mail: info@xyzpi.com
License #: C000100

Paint Colors
1._____
2._____
3._____
4._____
I approve the color(s) above:_____
(initials)

Choose XYZ Paint for all your painting needs!

SCOPE OF WORK

The work to be performed shall include, but is not limited to the following:

- Pressure wash all surfaces to be painted.
- Caulk all exposed cracks and holes around doors, windows, etc.
- Paint all drywall, wood trim, fascia, shutters, rain gutters and downspouts, pool fence, metal garage doors and handrails, wood fences and entry doors.

PAINT SPECIFICATION

Wood trim, fascia, shutters, rain gutters and downspouts
- Spot Prime: XYZ Primer
- One Coat: XYZ 100% Acrylic Paint Exterior Flat

Pool fence
- Spot Prime: XYZ Industrial Metal Primer
- One Coat: XYZ Industrial Water Base Alkyd Urethane Gloss

Wood garden fences
- Spot Prime: XYZ Deluxe Primer
- One Coat: XYZ Deluxe Paint Exterior Satin

Metal garage doors and handrails
- Spot Prime: XYZ Industrial Metal Primer
- One Coat: XYZ Industrial Water Base Alkyd Urethane Gloss

ACCEPTANCE OF SPECIFICATIONS

The above prices, specifications, and conditions are hereby accepted. Payments will be made as outlined above. I approve of the terms and conditions stated on reverse side.

Date of Approval:_____   Signature:_____   Signature:_____

Searching for Qualified Contractors: 3 is Key

*"Painting is easy when you don't know how,
but very difficult when you do."*

French artist Edgar Degas may not have been referring to painting drywall or stucco, yet it still applies. Essentially, anyone with a ladder and paint brush can call himself a painter; however, when it comes to undertaking an HOA job and dealing with hundreds of clients instead of one, only a skilled, reputable professional will do.

Making It Clear

Board members will create easy-to-understand SOWs if they…

keep sentences short.

limit each provision to three sentences.

use one term consistently to convey the contractor's obligations. (Example: "Contractor agrees to perform work…" and "Contractor agrees to deliver…")

avoid abbreviations, acronyms and words with special meanings.

eliminate ambiguous terms, such as "any," "either," "and/or" and "never."

One method for obtaining bids is a Request for Proposal (RFP), a general announcement that an organization, such as a community association, is interested in receiving bids for goods and services from quality providers. It's sent out with the SOW, information about the HOA and a request for information about the contractor that will help the association evaluate his capability to perform the work. Unlike a PS, RFPs don't necessarily require all contractors to bid on the same products, therefore, they almost always generate unequal bids that make it more complicated for HOAs to compare vendors.

Board members could also start their pursuit by gathering referrals from the property manager and searching the internet for industry experts with established presences in the area, web sites exhibiting job photos and reviews online. Next, HOA representatives may prescreen contractors by phone, inquiring about their qualifications. By collecting then verifying this information sooner than later, boards can eliminate unpleasant surprises at the eleventh hour. Companies unable or unwilling to supply proof of credentials and other data that's vital to the vetting process (see list opposite) should be promptly crossed off the list of contenders.

After preliminary due diligence, the selection committee typically whittles the list of qualified companies to the top three. Why? Two bidders aren't enough for comparison, and more is too many to manage in a timely fashion. Still, each state has different statutes regarding competitive bids and how many are required by HOAs. Board members should consult their governing documents, bylaws or HOA Declaration of Covenants, Conditions, and Restrictions (CC&Rs) to confirm.

During their search for contractors, board members will investigate and verify the following:

- **Business registration and/or license (requirements vary by state)-** Licenses can be confirmed online at: http://www.contractors-license.org/ or on a state's Department of Labor website by looking up the owner's or business name, license number or the type of license being verified. (In California, visit the Contractors State License Board at www.cslb.ca.gov or call 800-321-2752).

- **Workers' compensation and disability, and comprehensive general liability insurance-** Contractors must meet all minimum requirements. *Note:* The scope of the project determines how much insurance is needed.

- **Better Business Bureau (BBB) complaints-** The BBB may have records of grievances against the painting company.

- **An index of state and local consumer agencies-** Records of whether or not the contracting firm or its principals appear in litigation can be found at http://www.usa.gov/directory/stateconsumer/index.shtml.

- **References from similar jobs in size and complexity-** They help to weed out less suitable or inexperienced prospects. Small firms could be in over their heads when it comes to an extensive HOA project.

- **Professional affiliations-** Most certified painters join or become accredited by a national and/or local painting contractor's association or organization, such as the National Association of the Remodeling Industry (NARI) and the Painting and Decorating Contractors of America (PDCA), the largest painting contractor's association. In California, most qualified painting contractors belong to Community Associations Institute (CAI) and California Association of Community Managers (CACM).

Pre-emptive Pointers

Often serving as liaisons between the board and contractors for the duration of the work, good management plays a lead role in the search for skilled painters. Recognizing that HOAs deserve property managers who continually elevate their industry knowledge and job performance, Pacific Western Painting, Inc., offers educational material such as, "The 5 Mistakes Every Property Manager Must Avoid."

Walking the Site with Contractors

The difference between an adequate job and a great one is frequently determined while HOA representatives and the contractors -- collectively or individually – tour the work site. Depending upon the project, the property manager should schedule ample time for professionals to assemble the facts necessary for a thorough and accurate proposal. Contractors are expected to arrive on time, act professionally and review the prepared project specifications supplied by the board.

The walk provides an opportunity for managers to relay all pertinent information to potential contractors, including budget limitations, time constraints for submitting bids or completing the job, days and/or hours when work can and cannot be done, and logistical considerations. If board members have paint manufacturer preferences, the walk would be a good time to mention that and contractors should satisfactorily address all issues and requests in their proposals. During the walk, diligent providers will confirm, inspect and measure all substrates, ask questions and take notes. Some may describe their estimating process and many commonly request a second look around to gather final details.

Walking the site together not only affords both parties a chance to refine the scope of work, but also allows them to interact and get acquainted. Without an honest working relationship between provider and client, things will go downhill fast. It's advisable for HOA boards to consider a contractor's philosophy, commitment to quality, communication and trustworthiness.

What to Look (and Listen) for:

Properly screening contractors requires asking the right questions and then listening carefully to their responses. How is the candidate's demeanor, willingness to pinpoint and explain potential hazards? Does he offer reasonable alternative applications, materials or solutions that are cost-effective? Are answers professional and competent, or curt and lacking? Do direct questions receive direct answers? Is this someone who'd be easy to work with for the length of the project? When comparing contractors, boards may find that responses to these types of questions prove more critical than discovering which paint brand providers will use.

Parts of a Proper Proposal

After the top three painting contractors visit the work site and understand project objectives, they'll each submit a proposal. Vendors must provide a thorough, complete and accurate job specification, further defining the scope of work. Proposals may be delivered in person, sent certified mail, faxed or emailed.

While submissions may offer different approaches with similar results, they should all consist of the necessary components of the project, including the items on this helpful checklist for board members on the opposite page.

Site Map

Phase 1

Phase 2

Phase 4

Phase 3

- ■ Phase 1 (Buildings 1-4)
- ■ Phase 2 (Buildings 5-7)
- ■ Phase 3 (Buildings 8-10)
- ■ Phase 4 (Clubhouse/Gym)

General

___A further modified scope of work.

___Site map showing exact locations and dimensions of proposed work. (Sample on opposite page.)

___Proof of business license, adequate insurance and other credentials mentioned previously, if verification hasn't yet been done. If association administrators fail to verify coverage, it could ultimately leave residents liable for a worker's injury on the job.

___Assistance with HOA financing, if necessary.

___Arrangements regarding on-site restrooms for crew. Some HOA communities prefer that contractors use clubhouse facilities; others request on-site porta-potties, so placement should be considered, too.

Materials/Labor

___All deliverables essential for prep, work and cleanup and person(s) responsible for supplying.

___Identification of existing surface coatings and methods to remove, solutions for existing issues per phase.

___Party responsible for removing equipment, properly disposing of flammable materials and debris.

___Preferred relationships with major paint manufacturers.

Management/Staff

On-site foreman/primary contact:

___Able to communicate accurately and clearly; bilingual, if applicable.

___Available after hours and on weekends.

___Professional, experienced.

Crew:

___Adequate size to handle job within timeframe.

___Properly insured, bonded.

___Bilingual, if applicable.

___Properly vetted subcontractors, if applicable.

Quality Assurance/Risk Management

___Additional umbrella policy to insure full coverage, if applicable.

___3rd party safety training company.

Security/party responsible for:

___Equipment and material storage during non-working hours.

___Daily security clearance/check-in procedure for workers.

___Site access.

Technology/Communication

___Web communication available to notify HOA about progress updates, upcoming detours, etc.

___Easy access and prompt response time via email, phone and text.

___Online door appointment scheduler.

Contractor
1 2 3

Criteria

Criteria	1	2	3
Application	☐	☐	☐
Products	☐	☐	☐
Guidance/Solutions	☐	☐	☐
Warranty/Guarantee	☐	☐	☐
Price	☐	☐	☐
Philosophy	☐	☐	☐
Commitment to Quality	☐	☐	☐
Communication	☐	☐	☐
Insurance	☐	☐	☐
References from Similar Jobs/Testimonials	☐	☐	☐
Post-work Inspection/Maintenace Plan	☐	☐	☐
Add/Subtract Material Differences	☐	☐	☐
Overall Value/Totals	_____	_____	_____

Comparing Quotes

Once contractors submit proposals, the HOA's board of directors and property manager carefully review them, checking and double-checking that all project details have been adequately addressed. Not properly qualifying contractors is a mistake that no HOA – or any property owner – can afford to make.

Quotes may fall roughly within the same price range, but if they differ greatly, it's up to the selection committee to figure out why. Allowing for some comparability adjustments is to be expected. Still, if anything seems vague or suggests significantly altering the scope of work, contractors should clarify in writing. If follow-up information is required, board members should make every effort to find answers before proceeding. A contractor who fails to offer sound explanation should raise a red flag.

Comparing bids can be tedious, so board members may find that using the chart opposite, or one like it, will help furnish a framework for determining the overall value of painting contractors; a rating of 0, 1, 2 or 3 is assigned for each issue being assessed. Fields can be modified or added as needed.

See the Future with iScope

Pacific Western Painting, Inc. is the only Southern California painting contractor that provides HOA boards with "iScope," a visual scope of work. Presented via USB, digital copy, or CD-ROM, iScope offers HOA administrators an interactive, virtual preview of their actual community buildings *before, during* and *after* projected work is complete.

Screening the project's stages -- prepping, patching, painting, etc. -- in progress, reassures board members. No longer having to *imagine* the end result, they'll see exactly how the newly painted structures will look with iScope before deciding. PWP's exclusive web application also includes price quotes, references and other details routinely found in customary bids.

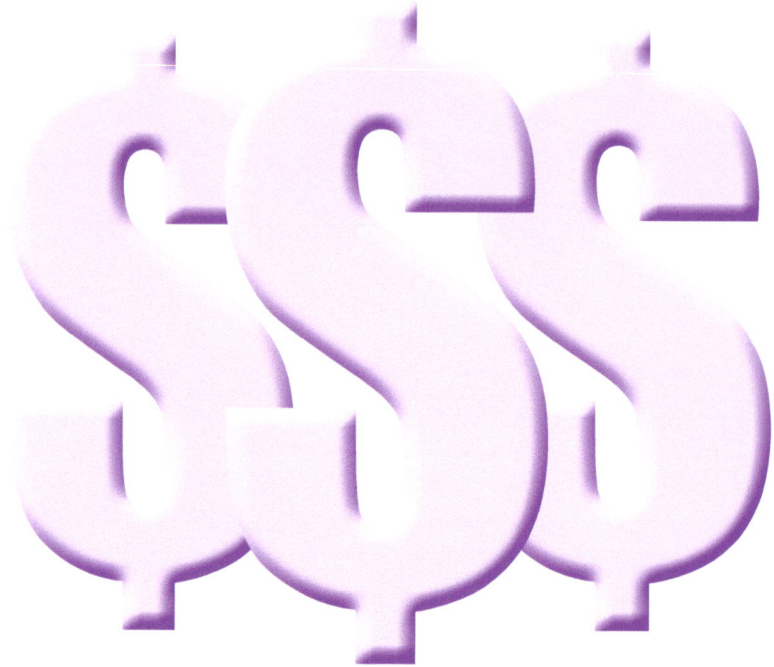

Price Is Negotiable, Quality Isn't

The cheapest bottom line may be tempting, but it shouldn't be the deciding factor. In fact, grabbing a "bargain" may prove costlier and sabotage a project's success. It's no secret that HOAs are considering other proposals, so it's possible – and not uncommon – for determined contractors to undervalue bids in hopes of landing the job. Unfortunately, underestimating invariably leads to change orders, cut corners, delays and more money after work has begun. A quality contractor should complete the job according to the contract, honoring the original price.

Still, negotiation is often part of the selection process. Although HOA administrators have a fiscal responsibility to their associations, price isn't necessarily an insurmountable barrier. An agreement can usually be reached when both parties are motivated and think collaboratively as partners in solving a common problem – structuring a contract that's mutually advantageous.

A Comprehensive Contract

A properly drafted, comprehensive contract between HOAs and painting providers ensures protection for both parties in the event of disputes. Proposals are fleshed out in even greater detail because the contract is the board's last chance to modify conditions and terms before work officially (and finally!) begins.

The board assumes the considerable task of protecting the association and property manager from liability against any claim, lawsuit, loss or expense as a result of the contract. With the help of HOA attorneys, boards and management are accountable for confirming that the contract clearly covers the elements of the refined SOW and any additional provisions including:

- Applicable codes, permits, manufacturer specifications and industry standards that have been met or will be, and the person(s) responsible for providing.

- Terms of all applicable product and labor warranties, and length of coverage.

- Final compensation for the work provided, including a periodic draw schedule and if necessary, the amount of retainage and terms upon which it may be released.

- Indemnification of all claims against association as a result of the contractor's performance, such as common area damaged during work, and attorney fees. (Some HOAs add a provision that parties meet and confer in good faith prior to the filing of any dispute resolution process, such as mediation, arbitration or litigation.)

- Notification of change orders and who may approve them.

- Resolution strategy for cost overruns after start date.

- Contractor promise to provide necessary lien waivers.

- Time frame for project completion, and contractor non-compliance penalties for delays past deadline.

- Some type of performance standard to fairly judge the quality of the contractor's work. In the painting industry, the Painting and Decorating Contractors of America Industry Standards are the measure by which the quality of wall coating work can be evaluated by the consumer.

- A default clause that identifies what constitutes a default or breach by either party.

Communication is Crucial

Before the project begins, association administrators together with the contractor will adopt a system that informs owners of progress, detours and parking restrictions while work is being done. A pre-project HOA meeting with the contractor to disseminate preliminary information, direct mailings, door-to-door notices or centrally located signage are ways to alert residents in advance about how work will affect them. Timely notifications per phase also often contain: site map(s) detailing work areas, start and completion dates and any special instructions that affect owners. Board members will also decide how much advance notice residents will require.

Following Up on the Follow-up

A professional painting contractor – and a good contract -- will incorporate a post-work inspection to identify and repair any issues, eliminating costly future problems. Pacific Western Painting's inspection plan is part of all its HOA jobs; the PWP contractor returns at 30-days, six months and one year to recheck materials and workmanship, and touch up areas if necessary.

Brush Up on Painting Basics: What HOAs Can Expect

Prep & Prime: It's All About That Base

"As my father taught me and my grandfather taught him, the most essential part of any painting project is preparation," says PWP principal Tony Hady. "It's in this process, not the actual application of paint, that true quality and longevity are created."

Painting begins only after preparation is complete. Common prepping processes that HOAs can expect include:

- **Safety -** Setting up cones, caution tape, barricades and detours that circumvent work areas in a secure and convenient manner is the first step to preparing an area.

- **Power (or Pressure) Washing -** All exterior substrates are power washed, which removes dirt and debris. Stained areas will require special attention during washing, but any necessary priming won't start until surfaces are thoroughly cleaned. Regardless of the type, surfaces also must be dry, in sound condition and contaminant-free to guarantee strong coating adhesion.

- **Masking -** Once surfaces are free of dirt and dust, masking begins. Lighting, signage, cars, windows and landscaping are covered with plastic and drop cloths to prevent overspray damage; masking tape is used to protect areas that won't be painted, then removed when the final coating dries.

- **Front and Exterior Doors -** Painting outside doors involves advance planning. Before painting or staining begins, doors are most often hand-sanded to clean, smooth and remove sheen, and hardware is masked with tape so it remains paint-free. During application and drying, front and exterior doors need to be kept open for about four to six hours (special stains may require two days of work) so it's not unusual that security and privacy become concerns for some owners. Accordingly, contractors should provide sufficient notice since most owners prefer to be home. The best time to schedule door painting is early morning, after hours or on weekends. Professional painting companies, such as PWP, now offer easy, online, door appointment scheduling to accommodate residents.

Prime Pointer

One of the reasons water gets trapped underneath a coating is because of substandard caulking. Expertly applying top-quality caulk is crucial for achieving a moisture-free finish.

Prime Examples

Primers smooth, seal, patch and prepare surfaces for painting and contribute to topcoat adhesion and longevity. They're recommended on most repaints, uneven surfaces, stripped or worn coatings and when moisture, extreme temperatures and humidity exist. Over time, tiny holes or cracks can seriously damage a finish's protective film by collecting water and cause peeling or rotting.

The type of priming and patching depends on the surface and its condition; there are countless products formulated for every problem and substrate, including wood, drywall, metal and masonry. The chart on the following pages contains the basic primer types and their purposes.

Prime or Repair With:

	What it is	**When to use**
Caulk	• A pliable primer-sealer that solidifies with air exposure. • Comes formulated for specific substrates. • "Non-paintable" caulk contains silicone and comes in clear and many colors. • Acrylic-latex "paintable" caulk holds paint, but must cure completely, at least 24 hours, or topcoat will flake.	• On exterior surfaces if caulk is specifically resistant to moisture, shrinkage and cracking. • To fill and seal gaps and holes less than a half-inch wide in walls or between molding and walls. • To seal dry joints between different surfaces, such as brick and wood. *Not recommended on joints or surfaces that flex during weather fluctuations because it'll crack.*
Joint Compound	• Also called "mud," "drywall compound" or "joint cement." • Available in powder, premixed paste and quick-set formula to minimize prep time. • Dry compound hardens rapidly -- 5 to 90 minutes depending on the brand; premixed takes about 24 hours. • May need several coats and sanding.	• To fill seams between drywall sheets and create smooth, even interior walls. • In conjunction with mesh or paper tape. • To cover panel joints, joint tape and fasteners. • To patch cracks, nail and screw holes. *Not recommended in high humidity or low temperatures, which affect drying times and application.*

Primer:

	What it is	When to use
Acrylic	• Binds paint uniformly to surfaces and dries quickly. • Varieties formulated specifically for interior or exterior, stain-, odor and moisture-resistance, and rust-inhibition. • Meets strict VOC regulations.	• To fill cracks on chalky areas and cover stains. • On plaster, bare drywall, soft woods, galvanized steel, iron, aluminum, bricks and concrete. • For best results of exterior flats and enamels. *Not recommended in extreme temperatures.*
Alkyd	• Waterproof; seals wood's porous surface, enabling topcoats to better coat and adhere. • Prevents or slows paint from peeling, cracking and blistering, and metal from rusting. • Dries slow and releases VOCs.	• On bare or painted wood, high-traffic areas, heavy use surfaces (doors, windows, cabinets) and most exterior substrates. • To prevent sap or tannin in wood, water and other stains from bleeding through topcoats. • For sealing nail heads and covering knots.
Bonding	• Penetrating, heavy-bodied, latex primer. • Provides smooth, durable surface for paint to absorb evenly. • No sanding and scraping before painting.	• For adhesion to challenging slick surfaces, such as PVC pipe, enamel and high-gloss finishes. • For bonding to rough or peeling drywall, wood, plaster, masonry, galvanized metal or aluminum.

What it is	When to use
Epoxy • Commonly used as an alkyd wood filler (must be formulated for that purpose). • Forms a repair stronger than the wood. • Thick, high-gloss protection against chemicals, rust and moisture, but tends to fade and yellow quicker when exposed to UV rays.	• On interior or exterior surfaces with more structural integrity, such as doors and door jambs, paneling, flooring, concrete and steel rain gutters, and on ferrous and non-ferrous metals. • To make a porous surface non-porous. • To cover knots and stains, and fill cracks on damp or dry surfaces.
High Build • Pricey, dense, acrylic primer-sealer. • Produces smooth wall surfaces, improving topcoat's application, sheen and durability. • Film thickens with each coat sprayed or rolled without running or sagging.	• To fill and cover minor drywall and cured plaster defects. • To level uneven, pitted and scratched surfaces, both painted and unpainted. • Under enamel, semi-gloss or gloss topcoats.
Shellac • Pigmented shellac used primarily as a primer-sealer for interior wood and masonry; exterior surfaces are limited to spot-priming. • Quick-drying; provides smooth, high-gloss surface and good adhesion between coats. • Excellent barrier against water penetration.	• To block and seal stains, such as water, rust, oil, smoke and grease, and odors, such as smoke, urine and nicotine from bleeding through finish. • On brick, cured plaster, ceiling tiles, stucco, paneling, plywood and painted surfaces. *Not recommended for wood that flexes with temperature changes; softens in direct sunlight.*

Putty:

Water-Based

What it is	When to use
• Pliable, latex wood filler available in many mixable colors to match stains.	• To fill nail holes, small gaps between mitered pieces, cracks, dents, splits and other defects on interior or exterior wood.
• Produces water-tight bond between wood.	
• Small repairs dry in about 2 hours, and larger areas can take up to 24 hours.	• Around window sills, paneling, cabinets, furniture, doors or baseboards.
• Sands easily.	• To smooth and level surfaces for topcoats.

What it is	When to use

Oil-Based

- Also called "painter's putty."
- Bears greater loads than latex putty.
- Slow drying and manageable longer.
- Can be smoothed as applied; no sanding.
- If the solvent bleeds through wood, spot priming is necessary.

- For interior or exterior surfaces.
- To fill and seal minor voids and cracks and smooth flaws in wood paneling and cabinets.
- To secure windows like glazing compound.

Not recommended as a surfacing compound.

Spackling

- Available in premixed paste or powder.
- Quality spackling is crack-, sag- and shrink-resistant.
- Accepts latex or oil topcoats.
- Prior to painting, it needs sanding.
- Drying times vary by type and brand.

- To fill holes, cracks, dents and minor defects in wood, drywall, plaster, brick, concrete and stucco.
- To even surfaces before painting on both interior and exterior surfaces; quick-drying lightweight spackling for indoors, and heavier type for varying climate outdoors.

Wood Grain Filler

- Also called "paste wood filler."
- Comes pre-tinted to match or tone down grain, or with stain or dye to add as needed.
- Latex filler holds stain easier, dries quickly and can be coated the same day.
- Oil-based filler needs 48 hours before coating, but usually only one application.

- To fill pores in "open-grained" woods, such as oak and mahogany, for an even finish and sheen.
- Only after surfaces are sanded and puttied to cover flaws, which grain fillers emphasize.
- For application before or after staining.

Paint: The Inside Story

Paint has essentially three components: pigments, particles that give paint its color and hide, or covering power; binders, or resins, the film-forming elements that bond ingredients together and provide adhesion to substrates; and solvents, chemical drying agents that cause paint to be liquid for application.

As paint dries, solvents evaporate leaving behind a hardened film composed of the remaining pigments and resins – most commonly acrylic in new paint technology, or alkyd, a synthetic resin being used less and less these days. Specialty paints also contain additives that supply these coatings with different properties, such as freeze- or mildew-resistance, depending upon their usage.

Virtually all interior and exterior paints fall into two general categories: solvent-based paints, also called oil-based or alkyds, and water-based latex paints. Oil-based paints contain a significantly higher level of organic solvents (see "Volatile Organic Compounds" on the next page). These solvents facilitate paint's application and drying, but also produce the noxious odor of freshly coated surfaces.

The trend these days is to use quality, water-based latex paint in which the solvent is water and much less hazardous. Water-solvent paint adheres well to exterior surfaces, dries quickly and prevents many paint failures. Now, improved water-based paints have virtually surpassed the longevity and durability of oil-based paints, too. In fact, oil-based paints are being phased out of use in the United States.

Nonetheless, new and old paint formulations can be confusing for laypeople. Some paint manufacturers refer to water-based paints as simply "latex," but products that may be labeled "latex" or "acrylic latex" don't actually contain any; instead, the binders are acrylic. Still, not all latex paints contain acrylic. Some contain different binding ingredients and fillers (ingredients that increase paint's volume), yet acrylic is considered superior and an indicator of high-quality paint.

Paint Contents

55 Gallon Drum

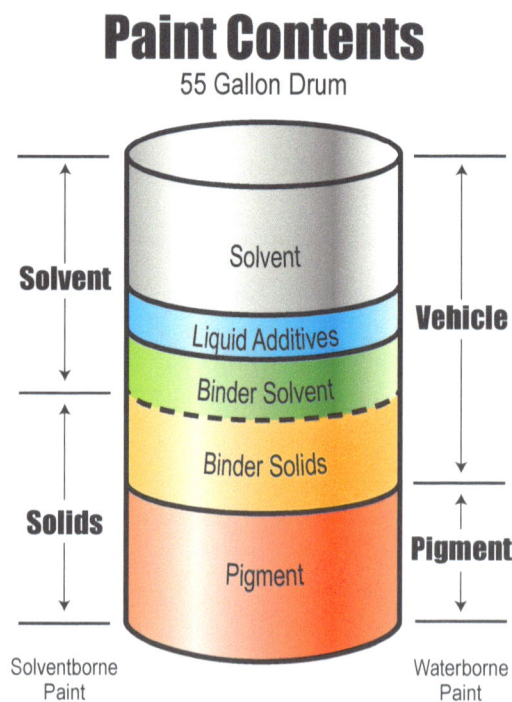

Solvent

Solids

Solvent
Liquid Additives
Binder Solvent
Binder Solids
Pigment

Vehicle

Pigment

Solventborne
Paint

Waterborne
Paint

Volatile Organic Compounds

"Volatile Organic Compounds" (VOCs) are any of several solvents, or chemical additives, found in numerous consumer products including paint. In paint, these chemicals get released into the air as coats dry, and exposure to this evaporation can result in mild- to serious, long-term health effects. Emission is greatest during and right after application, but continues at lower levels for months, emitting only half of its VOCs in the first year.

"VOC content" refers to the weight of volatile organic compounds per volume of product and is measured as grams per liter. To improve air quality, federal and state agencies have developed regulations to limit VOC emissions from solvent-containing products, requiring the installation of a control device, such as an incinerator, or the reduction of solvents in products.

Constantly evolving, VOC restrictions are being issued by more states, and the U.S. Environmental Protection Agency will soon mandate additional stringent national regulations. (For current California VOC regulations, visit the California Environmental Protection Agency at http://www.arb.ca.gov/coatings/coatingsrules.htm.)

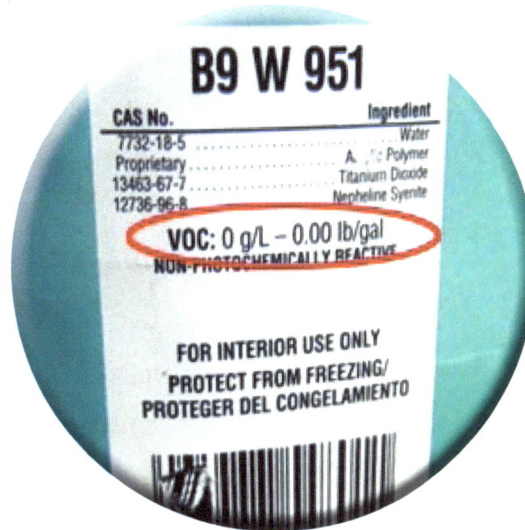

Did you know?

A simple way to find out if a paint is water- or solvent-based is by checking the label for directions about cleaning brushes. Oil-based paints require cleaning with solvents, and water-based paints need only warm, soapy water.

Paint Manufacturers Lean Toward Green

As the industry continues regulating VOC levels, paint manufacturers are illustrating compliance and promoting environmental awareness on their products. For example:

Green Seal Certified identifies and promotes green products and services by providing standards for low-VOC, anti-corrosive and recycled paints and adhesives.

Greenguard was founded to improve indoor air quality and reduce chemical exposure by developing guidelines and certifying low-emitting interior products.

MPI (Master Painters Institute) Green Performance® requires that all products meet or exceed the performance conditions of the applicable MPI product standard.

Scientific Certification Systems offers two levels of certification for paints and coatings, which must meet strict, indoor air-quality performance regulations to qualify.

Solvent Solutions

Today, water-based paints account for roughly 80 percent of architectural paints sold. Besides waterborne paints, advances in paint technology have also produced other alternatives to high-solvent coatings, such as high-solids paints. These newer premium paints contain approximately 30 percent solvents and 70-plus percent solids (what's left over after solvents evaporate), reversing conventional makeup of solvent-borne coatings, traditionally about 25 percent solids. The less solvent in paints, the higher the quality, better the coverage and lower the VOCs. High- solids coatings also entail less surface preparation and fewer coats, reducing cost per application.

Mainstream Myth:

Acrylic paint can be applied over oil-based paint on interior surfaces, but oil-based paint shouldn't be applied directly over acrylic without proper preparation and priming.

Despite declarations to the contrary saturating the Internet, water-based paint isn't recommended for application over oil-based paint unless it's properly prepared. Good quality acrylic paint will adhere just fine to old oil-based paint if the surface is first primed with an oil-based primer. If not, the acrylic topcoat will dry, but not adhere and peel right off the old oil-based paint, especially on exterior surfaces that flex in extreme temperatures*. Applying oil over oil creates better adhesion to surfaces, however, besides being phased out, oil paints eventually appear chalky and rapidly fade.

The following is a test that will help determine if the old coat is oil- or water-based:

First, scrub a small area with a solution of household detergent and warm water. Rinse well and towel dry. Next, soak a cotton ball, Q-tip or soft rag in alcohol and rub it back and forth over the cleaned area. If paint comes off, it's acrylic and another coat of the same is in order. If the paint does not come off, it's oil-based and the surface should be prepared with a primer to help with adhesion before applying acrylic paint. Once the primer dries, a water-based paint can be used successfully.

*Water-based paint applied on top of oil-based paint without proper preparation will peel or chip off before long.

No-Fail Paint Grades

More important than brand names are paint grades. Paint manufacturers make different grades of paints to meet application requirements, yet they basically come down to two main categories: premium, sometimes called professional, and economy, also called standard. The difference is the quality of ingredients.

Premium paints contain more solids, whereas economy brands are diluted with more liquids. Also, the high-grade binders found in premium varieties provide improved adhesion, color retention, film integrity and longevity.

Likewise, they resist dirt better than economy paint, hold up to frequent cleaning, spread easier, provide excellent coverage and require fewer coats.

Lower-quality economy paints offer good coverage, but lack durability, necessitate more coats and therefore, need maintenance sooner, especially on exterior substrates. Despite the higher price tag, top-grade paint means repainting less frequently and long-term savings for homeowners by extending the reserves. In short, it pays to use quality paints.

A House of a Different Color

HOA community colors should be aesthetically pleasing, suit the environment and complement exterior substrates, such as brick and stonework, and roof colors and styles. Colors that improve property value and won't go out of style quickly are best.

Board members must be able to rely on their painting professionals for color scheme recommendations and color samples, or "mock-ups," color options applied to a portion of a structure's exterior surface and allowed to dry. Hues appear differently depending upon the time of day, so mock-ups enable clients to view their choices on the actual substrates and feel confident before deciding.

Despite HOA parameters, color choice can be subjective, and when it comes to picking out hues for their homes, some owners feel it's downright personal. Under the best of circumstances, agreeing on a palette change is no simple undertaking for HOAs, so selecting colors while selecting a contractor isn't advisable. Accordingly, board members should allow ample time, six months to even a year prior to the anticipated project's start date, for potential decision-making delays.

A Feel For Quality

Although price is one strong indicator of grade, the "touch test" is another. After being stirred well, quality paint feels smooth and silky while standard types have a gritty feel. Less-expensive pigment materials, such as clay and talc, can't be ground as finely as the more costlier pigments giving those varieties their coarse texture.

Interior vs. Exterior Paint

There was a time when little differentiated interior from exterior paints, but with advancements in paint's chemistry, the new versions have become practically specialty products. Today, a primary difference between the two types is what binds the pigments to surfaces.

Exterior paint binders must be softer to accommodate fluctuating temperatures and chemically composed for durability so outside surfaces hold up to the harsh effects of sun, wind and water. Interior paint binders are more rigid to endure scuffing and scratching in high-traffic rooms and must contain low or even zero VOCs, withstand abrasion, clean easily and resist humidity and condensation in kitchens and bathrooms. Conversely, interior paints wouldn't survive long on a fence or other outdoor substrates regularly exposed to the elements because they lack vital weather-resistant additives, or agents. Although both oil- and water-based paints can be used indoors or outdoors, oils are often avoided for indoor work due to their unpleasant, possibly harmful odor and more challenging clean-up.

Sheen, or gloss level, refers to paint's degree of reflectivity and indicates another major difference between interior and exterior paints. The types of sheen, traditionally flat, eggshell, satin, semi-gloss and gloss, can either enhance a substrate's texture or emphasize its defects.

Durability is also affected -- the higher the sheen, the harder the paint and the easier to clean. Typically, all sheens can be used on a structure's interior or exterior, however, some are better suited for particular areas than others. Still, high-gloss finishes involve more surface preparation, are most difficult to apply and aren't necessary for all substrates. (See sheen chart on opposite page.)

A Painting Precaution

Sheens aren't necessarily consistent from brand to brand; for example, one manufacturer's satin may be glossier or flatter than another brand's.

Sheen	Description	Good Choice For
Flat, Matte, No-Sheen	Non-reflective, diffuses light, hides substrate imperfections, easiest to touch up, porous finish makes stain removal difficult	Low-traffic rooms, siding with cracks or imperfections, woodwork, fences, moisture-free stucco
Eggshell, Low-Sheen	Finish similar to the slight velvety sheen on an egg's surface, cleans better than flat	Living rooms, dining rooms, bedrooms, stucco
Satin, Low-Sheen	Pearl-like finish, holds up to light scrubbing with wet cloth, fade- and dirt-resistant, most universal	Moderate- to high-traffic areas, halls, kitchens*, bathrooms*, exterior walls, masonry
Semi-Gloss, Medium-Sheen (sometimes considered enamel)	Radiant sheen, reflects light directly, stain-, abrasion-, moisture- and mildew- resistant, easy to wash	High-moisture and traffic areas, doors, gutters
High-Gloss, High-Sheen (sometimes considered enamel)	Glass-like finish, brightens rooms, most durable, least porous, mildew-resistant, needs most prep, magnifies flaws, easiest to clean	Window trim, shutters, handrails, architectural details, exterior doors

*For the past decade, interior designers have been recommending less sheen for these high-moisture areas.

Enamels &
Elastometric
Coatings

Enamels:

Historically, the term "enamel" has been used to describe oil-based paints with glossy finishes; however, because of the tremendous popularity of water-based alternatives, today most high-quality, hard-surfaced, high-sheen paints are commonly referred to as enamels. New waterborne enamels are now used customarily in place of oils on base boards, doors, door jambs, window sills, crown molding, cabinets and heavy usage areas.

The updated indoor options appear and react like oil-based paints, holding up to repeated washing and abrasion while providing excellent coverage, color retention, quicker drying and lower VOC levels without yellowing after time – a common problem with previous solvent-borne enamels. Newer exterior semi- and high-gloss enamels are composed to be highly elastic, expanding and contracting in varying temperatures without splitting or compromising adhesion. Acrylic enamels also offer low-temperature, rust-, rot-, moisture- and heat-resistant application properties for defense against outdoor environments.

Elastometric Coatings:

Designed for exterior masonry surfaces like concrete and stucco, and to be applied in very thick coats, elastomeric coatings are about 10 times denser than other paints. Though tough, they're particularly known for their flexibility, or stretchiness, which can handle substrate movement, bridging cracks and keeping water out without affecting adhesion. Accordingly, elastomeric coatings are excellent for waterproofing surfaces and much like wrapping a structure in plastic.

Undeniably, elastomeric coatings have many excellent properties, but they're also higher in material and labor costs since the spread rate (the area to which paint can be spread) is reduced to approximately 30 percent of conventional exterior paints. Because they're softer and mastic, or pasty, they attract dirt, so achieving a uniform finish usually requires experienced technicians; failure usually comes from poor preparation, improper application, the wrong product type or an incompatible substrate. Accordingly, only contractors proficient in its use should be consulted on whether or not an elastomeric coating is the best choice for specific surfaces. Kinds of elastomeric coatings include acrylic, butyl, polyurethane and silicone.

A Sure Cure for Moisture

The rate at which solvents evaporate differs between latex and oil paints and depends on the denseness of coats, surface, sheen, ventilation, humidity and temperature. Latex paint dries from the outside in and looks dry quickly after application; although surfaces may even feel dry, too, they could still be wet within, especially when applied to porous surfaces like bare wood and masonry. That's because latex cures through coalescence, a process when pigments and binders fuse together into a dry, durable film during evaporation. Curing means that paint has reached maximum hardness and is 100 percent moisture-free.

Oil-based paint dries from the surface area out allowing for a stronger bond with substrates. Even so, when solvents have evaporated only from the paint's surface, the film remains vulnerable to staining, scratching and damage from water and chemicals; in fact, pressing a fingernail into it will leave a mark, an indicator that paint hasn't cured yet.

Oil cures by oxidation. After solvent evaporation, the binders oxidize, or react with oxygen, creating a hard film When the coated substrate can withstand minor scratches, bumps and cleaning without damage, it has fully cured.

Adequate ventilation is another critical aspect of drying and curing. As paint films dry, the surrounding air becomes saturated with the evaporating moisture or solvents; without a breeze those saturated molecules don't move and therefore, drying slows.

What's more, dampness not only in the air but also in the unpainted surfaces slows curing, interferes with adhesion and shortens paint's longevity. Generally, substrate moisture content must be below 15 percent for proper bonding and curing; for example, a safe moisture content for painting wood shingles and clapboards is 12 percent or below, and concrete moisture levels should be 2 percent or below. Surface temperature can even vary on the same structure further interfering with the application and drying times. With the help of hand-held moisture meters, contractors can assess a substrate's wetness level before starting to coat.

Info to go

Both product information (PI) sheets and safety data sheets (SDS) are available for all paint products. PI sheets supply ideal temperatures and acceptable levels of moisture in the air and surfaces for application, and any instructions that ensure paints dry and cure at their optimal pace to create enduring finishes. The air, paint and surface to be coated must fall within recommended application temperature ranges for coatings to cure properly. An SDS lists additional safety information and handling instructions for paints and stains.

Why Wait?

"Recoat" and "use" times can usually be found on paint cans and PI sheets. The recoat time is the manufacturer's recommended amount of time that the coating must dry before a second layer can be applied without compromising the finish. The use time is the time that paint must be allowed to cure before objects can be placed on a surface without leaving imprints.

The time frames below are based on optimal temperature ranges.

Stage of Dry:	Acrylic Paint	Oil-Based Paint
Dry (to touch)	2 hours	4-10 hours
Recoat	24 hours	24 hours
Use	2-4 Weeks	3-4 Days

Weather or Not to Paint

An exterior paint project can be destroyed by varied weather. Hot temperatures especially cause painting failures, such as cracking sealants and films that develop blisters, moisture bubbles trapped beneath the coating. Blisters lift paint from underneath, requiring surfaces to be scraped or sanded, then re-primed before repainting. Painting in cooler temperatures can cause improper film development, poor color uniformity, inadequate stain resistance, reduced coverage and longer drying time.

The adhesion of latex paint is dependent on its water base evaporating and low temperatures impede that process; at high temperatures, latex will dry too quickly to brush out properly. Oil-based paints are more forgiving than latex in this regard, but lower temperatures will still hinder drying times.

Substrates not only become moist by rain, snow or humidity, but they can also get hotter or colder than the surrounding temperature, inhibiting paint from flowing uniformly or drying and curing properly. Both quickening and slowing the drying process weaken bonds between paints and surfaces, generate cracking and peeling, and shorten a coating's lifespan.

Until recently, industry standards dictated that ambient temperatures must stay above 50°F with a relative humidity of 50 percent or less in order for paints and stains to achieve adequate application and drying. Yet, as paint quality improved over the years, so did the minimum temperature point, and manufacturers now offer products that can be applied in as low as 35°F. In extreme temperatures, contractors now may choose to either postpone painting or use specially formulated exterior paint that cures beyond average temperatures.

Expert painting contractors abide by the following exterior painting protocol:

- Paint application should be avoided if temperatures are predicted to drop below the recommended minimum anytime within the next 36 hours.

- Fall is traditionally a good season for painting since day and evening temperatures vary less than other times of the year; temperature fluctuations can be detrimental to application and drying.

- Sunlit surfaces can reach 20 degrees above the air temperature.

- In general, exterior latex paint shouldn't be applied immediately after a rain or during foggy weather. In damp climates, moisture penetrates paint film and prevents topcoats from bonding with undercoats or surfaces, which results in peeling.

- A latex paint with all-acrylic binders has superior weather-resistance and can extend painting season by as much as two months in some climates.

- Painting should cease at least eight hours before anticipated showers, and be postponed 24 - 48 hours after a storm.

- Condensation can rehydrate incompletely dried paint films and prompt coatings to run.

- Depending upon the concentration of shade surrounding a structure, paint may need an extra day or two to dry. Similarly, pressure washing in cold climates should be avoided because it'll take longer for surfaces to thoroughly dry.

- Like sun, wind speeds up paint's drying time, triggering cracks and weakening adhesion. Windy conditions also stir up dust, dirt, pollen and other contaminants that impair paint finishes and can cause an average 25-percent paint loss from overspray.

Did you know?

This simple "sidewalk test" is used by professional painters to help them determine the dryness of exterior surfaces: If it rained the day before, but the pavement is dry, the building's substrates are probably dry, too. Rain doesn't commonly saturate siding, which is often protected by roof overhangs.

A Brush With Problematic Paint

Exterior painting failures can be stubborn or difficult to address, but most are correctable. Here are some common paint problems, their causes and solutions.

ALLIGATORING

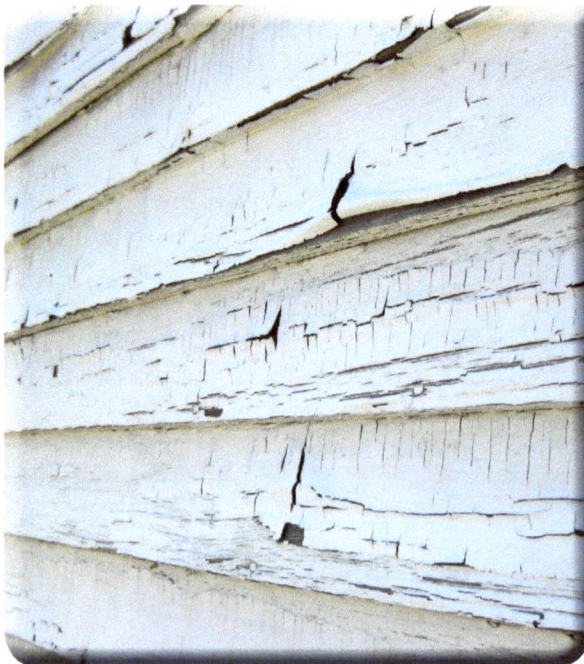

Appearance:
Small vertical and horizontal cracks resembling alligator skin.

Causes:
Too many layers of paint; a second coat of paint applied over a not fully dry base coat; temperature changes that cause substrates to expand and contract.

Solution:
Paint should be stripped off; otherwise it will continue to crack through the new coat, too.

CHALKING

Appearance:
A fine chalky oxidized powder that forms on paint film; typically found on masonry.

Causes:
An inadequately primed and sealed substrate; low-grade or incompatible paint; sun exposure; over-thinned paint.

Solution:
Power wash or scrub to remove, dry thoroughly and repaint with better quality paint.

EFFLORESCENCE

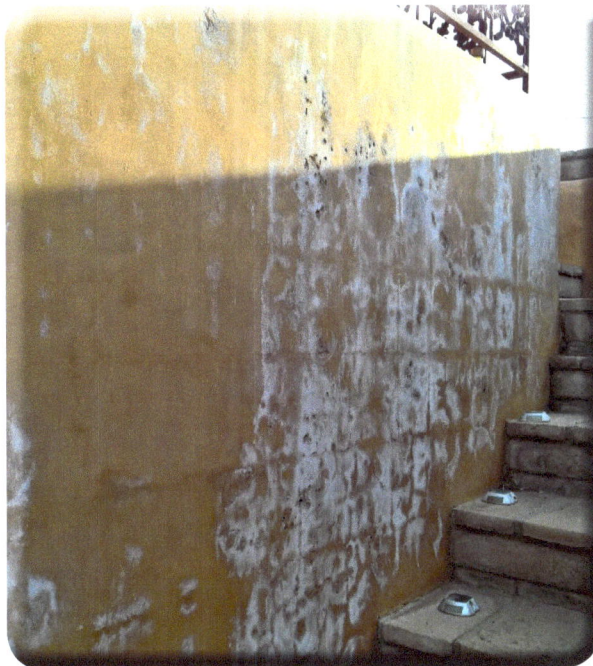

Appearance:
Crusty, white salt deposits that push up through the paint film.

Causes:
Poor surface preparation or heavy substrate moisture.

Solution:
Power wash and dry thoroughly, scrape with a wire brush before patching cracks with caulk or apply waterproofing to exterior wall before repainting with premium paint.

LAPPING

Appearance:
Lap marks present as a denser color or higher gloss where wet and dry layers overlap.

Causes:
Wet and dry layers intersect during application; paint applied in direct sunlight or on porous surfaces; failure to maintain a wet edge when painting; using a low-solids economy paint.

Solution:
Using a top-quality, water-based paint, apply a uniform topcoat by brushing or rolling from wet to dry rather than vice versa.

SAGGING or RUNNING

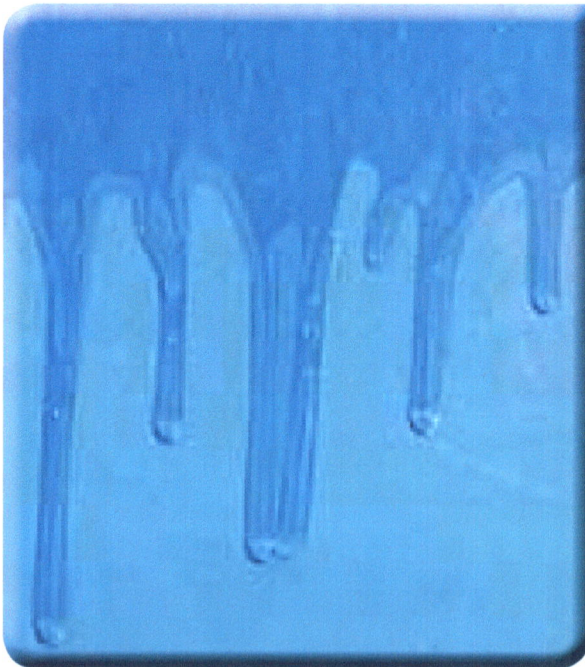

Appearance:
Paint film appears to be dripping or drooping.

Causes:
Heavy application; over-thinned paint; coats applied in extreme weather; improperly cleaned or primed substrate.

Solution:
Wet paint should be immediately brushed or re-rolled to redistribute excess evenly; paint that has dried needs sanding and a new coat, or two lighter coats of quality paint.

SKINNING

Appearance:
Film on the surface of paint that's in the can.

Causes:
Paint can lids become warmer than the contents; that temperature imbalance causes evaporation of any paint on a lid and condensation on the cooler surface of paint in the can.

Solution:
Use paint with anti-skinning agents and keep out of direct sunlight. Sometimes, straining paint through a nylon bag or filter before repainting will resolve the problem, however, skin could disperse into countless tiny lumps making the paint unsalvageable.

Painting by Numbers

"Close to 100% of paint failures are due to technician error," says PWP's Tony Hady. "And, 75% of a successful paint job is due to proper substrate preparation before painting."

The Truth about Touch-ups

Reducing oil-based paint by 10 to 15 percent with a proper thinner that's recommended by the paint manufacturer, may help touch-up paint blend with original paint.

High-gloss finishes are particularly difficult, and the slightest sheen difference results in touch-up failure.

If there's more than a 15-degree temperature difference between the times that painting and touch-ups are done, slight color and sheen variations will result. Replicating the exact conditions that existed when surfaces were originally painted and stirring paint thoroughly will increase the odds of success.

Priming repaired areas results in optimal paint adhesion and color blending. The size of the primed area should be confined to the dimensions of the repair and dried thoroughly for best results. Without primer, the touched-up spot will stand out.

There's no such thing as a perfect touch-up unless it's repainted from corner to corner of the surface. Waiting over a month to touch-up areas decreases the chance of success on stucco, drywall and other substrates.

When fresh paint is applied over old paint of the same color, colors will appear different until the surface cures. Checking the match at different angles and in both natural and artificial light at different times of the day help painters determine outcomes.

Storing touch-up paint in the smallest container possible will extend its life; any remaining air in it will cause paint to go bad sooner.

Lead Has Left the Building Industry

Structures built after 1978 are less likely to contain lead-based paints since the Environmental Protection Agency (EPA) has classified lead and inorganic lead compounds as "probable human carcinogens." Removal of old paint by sanding, scraping or other means may generate dust or fumes that contain lead, and exposure may cause adverse health effects, especially in children and pregnant women.

If lead-based paints are suspected on a project, all removal must be done in accordance with the EPA's Renovation, Repair and Painting Rule, or state and local regulations. Dealing with hazardous substances requires proper protective equipment, containment and cleanup. For more information, call the National Lead Information Center at 1-800-424-LEAD. Upon request, most painting contractors will provide residents with material about preventing contact during renovations.

Tools of the Painting Trade

Professional painting contractors use commercial-grade power washers for large jobs. Today's commercial machines clean with cold water, hot water or steam and the pressure they deliver to substrates is expressed in pounds per square inch (PSI). Power washers with 3000-5000 PSI sufficiently break bonds between dirt, grime and the surfaces, stripping paint, removing heavy grease stains, persistent concrete spots and more; however, using the wrong technique, pressure, tip or cleaning agent will damage certain surfaces.

One of the most common homeowner questions about current, exterior painting techniques regards the widespread use of automatic, or pneumatic, sprayers. In the past, homes were painted with brushes and rollers, and though they're still used for detail work, automatic sprayers have many advantages. Since they decrease the time it takes to paint one house from weeks to days without sacrificing quality, using a power sprayer also decreases labor and the number of painters needed per job. Furthermore, the correct use of a pneumatic paint sprayer results in smoother, more uniform coats with less runs and blemishes than brushes and rollers, which means less paint and wastage and more savings for homeowners.

Other equipment includes the following aerial work platforms to access tall exteriors:

- **Boom Lift:** an elevated platform or bucket at the end of a hydraulic lifting system, also known as a cherry picker, man lift, basket crane or hydra-ladder.

- **Swing Stage (opposite):** a scaffold that's suspended by ropes or cables from the roof, and can be raised or lowered to any height.

- **Scissor Lift:** a type of platform that usually only moves vertically with the use of linked, folding supports in a crisscross "X" pattern, known as a pantograph, or scissor mechanism.

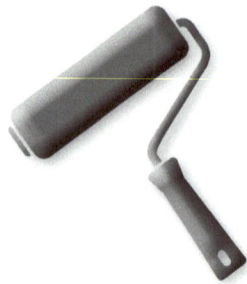

More Area to Cover

The proper finish adds longevity to the appearance of any interior or exterior substrate, particularly wood. Different finishes have varying degrees of aesthetics, durability, ease of application, protection and reparability, and selecting one is often a tradeoff. Likewise, depending upon the wood type, porosity and whether it's bare or stained, finishes react differently. All finishes, however, call for warm, dry conditions.

The following chart lists common topcoats and their distinguishing qualities.

Finish:

Lacquer

A solvent-based, moisture-resistant and more durable alternative to varnish, lacquer is used on cabinetry, and other interior wood. The clear or colored, highly flammable coating comes in several sheens. It sprays on evenly without sagging or running, dries quickly, and is easy to recoat and repair.

Note: Applying in high humidity or temperatures can cause a milky finish.

Types:

Nitrocellulose
- traditional lacquer
- moderate protection and durability
- the solvent evaporates, forming a hard yet flexible, smooth film
- each thin coat dissolves and blends with the previous one
- good color retention

Pre-catalyzed
- contains acrylic resins
- better abrasion, chemical and stain resistance than nitrocellulose lacquer
- a catalyst is added at the factory, so it comes ready to use
- longer drying time
- pot life about six months

Finish:

Polyurethane

Extremely hard, thick, durable polyurethane comes in many sheens for wood and metal surfaces. One of its major benefits is its resistance to heat and flames. It's easy to brush, spray or wipe on high-wear, moisture-prone surfaces, such as tabletops, hardwood floors, doors, windows, shutters and cabinets, and can be formulated for interior or exterior use; generally requires 2-3 coats.

Types:

Colored 2-part high-performance

- optimal protection against abrasions, chemicals and water on metal
- a base coating (part A) and a catalyst or chemical (part B) are combined before use initiating a chemical reaction
- retains color and gloss longer
- costs more than 1-part coatings

Oil-based

- imparts an amber glow
- excellent abrasion, chemical, stain and water resistance
- requires fewer coats and lasts longer
- easy to apply, but long recoat time
- strong odor initially
- causes yellowing of white paint

Water-based

- improved, but less durability
- doesn't penetrate wood, so quicker drying
- difficult to repair
- accents wood's natural character without the amber tint
- minimal VOCs, low odor, easy clean up
- costs twice as much as other types

Finish:

Varnish

A clear protective finish that can be tinted, varnish is used on bare or stained surfaces, such as furniture and floors; sheens vary from flat to high gloss. Varnishes are differentiated by the varying amounts of oil, resin, solvent and drying agent they contain. Applied by brush or spray, they can be more difficult to apply than some other finishes, requiring multiple coats.

Types:

Oil-based
- the most common interior varnish
- less-expensive, durable protection
- enhances wood's depth and color
- 24-hour recoat time
- not as transparent as lacquer

Water-based
- durable and doesn't crack, chip, bubble or yellow
- easier to apply and clean up
- needs fewer coats
- generally dries clear to the touch in 15-30 min
- low-odor

Conversion
- high quality, transparent and quick-drying
- high build with fewer coats
- requires adding a catalyst before use for performance benefits
- excellent durability and resistance to heat and moisture
- chemical cure makes repairs difficult
- short pot life

Spar
- high-gloss, durable and flexible in extreme weather
- contains UV blockers for use on exterior wood doors, window sills and trim
- eventual chipping or chalking requires reapplication
- 24-hour recoat time
- needs several thin coats

Finish:

Stain

Available in clear or colors, stain maintains wood's natural features. Opacity ranges from translucent to solid, subject to pigment content; the more pigment, the more masking and durability. Still, since wood absorbs stain, no protective barrier forms, leaving it susceptible to water and UV damage. Results depend on the color, wood type and porosity, and the time between application (by brush or rag) and removal of the excess before it dries. Spot testing is recommended.

Types:

Oil-based

- more protection on outdoor surfaces, such as decks and fences
- penetrates wood slowly without raising the grain
- longer drying time
- strong odor and higher VOCs
- requires less upkeep and touches up easily

Water-based

- odorless and breathable
- bonds well to many surfaces
- quick dry and easy cleanup
- comes in more colors and retains color better
- raises wood grain so sanding is necessary after stain dries
- best choice for mildew-prone areas and coastal homes

Exterior

- generally solvent-based
- contains additional abrasion, fade and mildew resistors that tolerate extreme climate on substrates, such as siding and decks

Interior

- generally waterborne
- enhances color and texture of wood on doors, door and window trim, beams and floors
- a clear polyurethane or varnish topcoat is often applied
- more prep needed

Paint vs. Fog Coat

Many homes and communities especially in the Southwest are built with an exterior stucco finish. If stucco has no signs of defects and blemishes, then fog coating, (the application of a pigmented, bonding cement that coats existing stucco), may provide an economical option to painting, but it isn't necessarily the best.

Stucco is a porous surface, which makes it susceptible to cracking, fading and mildew, and if not properly protected with sealing properties like the ones found in paint, moisture will be readily absorbed compromising the structure's integrity. Additionally, fog coat is not recommended for painted and smooth surfaces, metal or sealed wood, so its uses are more limited than paint's. Exterior stucco is better protected with a quality, flat acrylic paint, which besides having the lowest VOC levels also prolongs the substrate's life.

Paint vs. Fog Coat

	Paint	Fog Coat
Aesthetics	durable, even-colored appearance	initially refreshes the look, but discolors unevenly and ages quicker
Cleaning	remains cleaner over a longer period of time	porous surface traps dirt and is prone to staining
Maintenance/ Touch-Ups	easy repair, touch-up and color matching	requires spraying to repair discolorations making precise color matching more difficult
Color	premium paints are available in any color	for similar colors only
Mildew Resistance	breathable, allows moisture to escape then run off or evaporate and quickly dry	no chemical composition to resist moisture, acts like a sponge when wet
Longevity	under optimal conditions adhesion lasts 5-10 years, possibly longer with premium paint	may adhere as long, but discolors and fades faster
Sealing	contains sealing properties that form a barrier between stucco and moisture	contains no sealing properties
Peeling	peels prematurely only if an underlying construction or severe moisture issue compromises coating	Peels easily if substrate isn't thoroughly dry or when applied improperly

What's in Storage?

Part of a complete painting job includes tidying up the site and storing leftover products. Contractors know that improper storage shortens shelf life, and painting products, such as flammable solvents, stains and spray paints, can spontaneously combust if dumped directly into the trash.

The key is to keep cans entirely air-free. The smallest opening will allow air to enter and leave altering a product's chemistry and effectiveness. Can lids should be free of paint or stain residue in their rims, or chimes, and sealed tightly. Storage temperature should be comfortably above 32°F since the freeze-thaw cycle will ruin paint. Conversely, paints and stains shouldn't be stored in direct sunlight, inside a hot attic or garage, or next to something warm, such as a water heater or furnace because heat also accelerates deterioration. Inadequate storage can be costly, too. For example, the loss of paint due to skinning, which happens most often due to overheating in storage, is estimated to be as much as 3 to 5 percent.

Paint longevity can vary slightly, so checking paint's texture and smell before reusing is always recommended; if it smells like rotten eggs (even if it looks fine) the paint is spoiled and the odor will remain even after application. The following chart illustrates how long common painting materials will generally last when properly stored and sealed.

Products	Opened	Unopened
Water-Based (Latex) Paint	1 Year	2 Years
Oil-Based Paint	1 Year	1 Year
Water-Based Stain	1 Year	2 Years
Oil-Based Stain	1 Year	2-3 Years
Glazing Compound	1 Year	2 Years
Oil-Based Varnish	1 Year	1 Year
Caulk	2 Months	1 Year
Water Putty	1 Year	1 Year

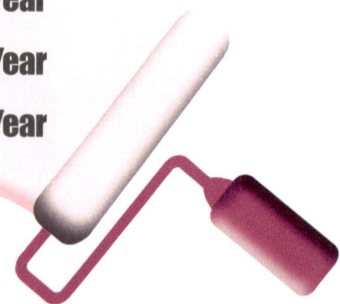

Post-Consumer Paint Management:

An estimated 10 percent of the more than 650 million gallons of architectural paint sold annually in the United States is unused. That staggering number also represents the largest portion of local household hazardous waste.

Post-consumer paint can be stored and reused, recycled, used for energy recovery (any process that converts waste material into energy) or safely disposed of, but doing so requires consumer education. That's why the American Coatings Association (ACA) created PaintCare®, a not-for-profit organization committed to reducing the generation of post-consumer paint by focusing on reusing options, helping consumers buy the correct amount of paint initially and providing an online paint calculator.

ACA and its industry maintain that manufacturers do not produce paint to be thrown away or recycled, but to be used up. Paint that's stored improperly not only goes bad quickly, but also can release toxic fumes. When it's disposed of improperly, it can end up contaminating the water supply or igniting a fire.

Glossary

ABRASION-RESISTANT: A property in a specially formulated coating that protects substrates against wear, or being worn away by rubbing or friction; related more to toughness than to hardness and is an essential feature of enamels, floor finishes, and varnishes.

ABRASIVE: Used for wearing away a surface by rubbing, scraping and sanding in preparation for coating; examples include sandpaper and steel wool.

ACRYLIC: A synthetic resin used in high-performance, water-based coatings.

ADDITIVES: Chemical agents used to modify and improve a paint's properties depending on where and how the coating will be used; for example, additives in exterior paint can help ptotect against water, rust, extreme temperatures, mold and mildew.

ADHESION: The ability of a coating to stick to a surface.

AIR DRY: One method by which liquid coatings dry; after solvent evaporation, the binders react with oxygen, or oxidize, creating a hard film.

AIRLESS SPRAY: An applicator that pumps paint at a very high pressure through a hose with a tip designed to spray contents evenly in a fan-shaped pattern, covering more area quickly.

ALKALI: A substance such as lye, soda or lime that can be highly caustic or corrosive to paint films.

ALKYD: Any of a group of synthetic resins that are used in varnishes, paints and adhesives; a paint in which the vehicle is an alkyd resin.

ALLIGATORING: A paint failure that appears like small cracks resembling alligator skin due to too many coats, a topcoat applied to a partially dry basecoat, or temperature changes that cause substrates to expand and contract.

ANTI-CORROSIVE: A property of a specially formulated paint or primer that inhibits corrosion on iron, steel and other metallic substrates. See Corrosion-Inhibitive.

BACK PRIMING: The application of paint to the backs of surfaces, such as exterior shingles, siding or trim to help prevent moisture from permeating.

BARRIER COAT: A layer of a primer or finish that obstructs or prevents passage of water or other contaminants through a surface. See Intermediate Coat.

BINDER: A main component of paint that joins pigment particles together into a cohesive film after the solvent evaporates, enabling paint adhesion to surfaces; it determines many film properties such as gloss, durability, and drying time. See Resin.

BLEACHING: The process of lightening or restoring discolored or stained wood to its normal color.

BLEEDING: A coating failure in which soluble dyes or pigments in an undercoat are dissolved by topcoat solvents and stain through the finish.

BLISTERING: When bubbles or pimples form on a painted surface because of excessive heat, or a premature topcoat applied to a partially dry undercoat. Also called bubbling.

BLUSHING: A common finish failure, especially in lacquers, that occurs when solvents evaporate in high humidity and moisture gets trapped below the coating's film; surfaces appear cloudy or dull.

BODY: The consistency of a coating. See Viscosity.

BOXING: Mixing paint by pouring from one container to another several times to ensure a consistent, well-blended color.

BREATHE: The ability of a paint film to permit moisture permeation without causing failure.

BRIDGING: The ability of a paint to cover or stretch over cracks, voids or other small gaps.

BRISTLES: The natural (usually hog) or artificial (nylon or polyester) stiff hairs at the end of a paint brush; natural bristles are best for applying oil-based paints, and synthetic bristles are recommended for water-based paints.

BRUSHABILITY: The ability or ease with which paint can be brushed onto a surface.

BRUSH-OUT: A technique that consists of applying a sample of paint to a piece of wood or other material, illustrating the finished surface.

BUILD: Thickness or depth of a paint film.

BURNISHING: To make smooth or glossy by rubbing.

CALCIMINE: A thin, water-based white or tinted wash containing zinc oxide, glue and coloring that's applied to interior plaster surfaces, such as walls and ceilings. Also called kalsomine.

CATALYST: An additive for paint that accelerates drying time and durability.

CAULKING COMPOUND: A slow-drying, flexible sealing material used to fill or close gaps in structures, seal joints and fill crevices around windows, chimneys and most surfaces. Also called sealant.

CEMENTITIOUS COMPOSITION BOARD: A versatile, durable and affordable exterior building material that's more stable than wood or plywood; mimics all-natural wood siding, but unlike wood, doesn't rot or become infested with parasites such as termites. Also called fiber cement board.

CHALKING: The formation of a loose powder on the surface of paint after exposure to the elements.

CHECKING: A paint failure characterized by narrow cracks or splitting in the paint film's surface that's a result of overly thick or excessive coats.

CHROMA: The purity or intensity of color; a color at its full intensity has maximum chroma.

CLEAR COATING: A transparent protective and/or decorative film.

COALESCENCE: The process whereby water evaporates from a coating, forcing pigments and binders to fuse together into a dry, durable, continuous film.

COATING: A layer of paint, varnish, lacquer or other finish used to create a protective and/or decorative layer.

COHESION: The attraction of molecules within a coating that's required for a durable film.

COLORANT: A dye, pigment or other substance that when added to coatings causes a color change.

COLORFAST or COLOR-RETENTIVE: A fade-resistant property in paint specially formulated for exposure to the elements or repeated washings.

COLOR UNIFORMITY: Describes the non-variation in a coating's color across its entire surface, and from light source to light source.

CONVERSION COATING: Provides metals with a protective layer that results from the chemical action between the coating and surface, and aids in adhesive bonding.

COPPER STAINING: An aesthetic problem caused by the corrosion of copper items, such as screens or chimney flashing, washing down onto and staining painted surfaces.

CORROSION-INHIBITIVE: A property in a specialty coating formulated to prevent rust by blocking moisture from reaching metal surfaces. See Abrasion-Resistant.

COVERAGE: The surface area concealed by coating, expressed usually in square feet per gallon or square meters per liter.

CRACKING: A type of paint failure characterized by the splitting or breaking of a dry coating that worsens over time, and is caused by poor preparation, cheap paint or repainting before the previous coat thoroughly dries.

CRAWLING: A defect in freshly applied paint or varnish characterized by bare patches and ridging.

CRAZING: Small, interlacing cracks that appear when two materials bonded together (e.g., substrate and primer, or primer and basecoat) expand or contract at different rates, severing surface adhesion.

CURING: When paint film has reached maximum hardness and is 100 percent moisture-free.

CUSTOM COLOR: A unique color created by mixing colorants.

CUTTING IN: The technique of precisely painting an edge, such as the ceiling line or the edge between a wall and molding.

DELIVERABLES: A term for the quantifiable goods or services that will be provided by contractors and vendors upon the completion of a project.

DILUENT: A liquid, such as turpentine, that reduces the viscosity of paint or varnish making it easier to apply. Also called reducer, thinner, reducing agent or reducing solvent.

DRAWDOWN CARDS: Black and white plastic cards supplied by retail stores, which provide accurate color and sheen levels of the paints being considered; a small amount of paint is spread onto cards by a metal drawdown bar eliminating brushstrokes and roller marks.

DRY COLOR: A pigment in powder form that's added to paint.

DRY DUST FREE: The stage of drying when particles of dust that settle upon the surface don't stick to the paint film.

DRY TACK FREE: The stage of drying when the paint no longer feels sticky or tacky to the touch.

DRY TO HANDLE: The stage of drying when a paint film has hardened sufficiently so the surface may be used without marring. Also called use time.

DRY TO RECOAT: The stage of drying when the next coat can be applied.

DRY TO SAND: The stage of drying when a paint film can be sanded without the sandpaper sticking or clogging.

DURABILITY: The ability of paint to hold up well against destructive agents such as weather, detergents, air pollution or abrasion.

DYE or DYESTUFF: A natural or synthetic agent used for permanently changing the color of something.

EGGSHELL FINISH: A degree of gloss that's similar to the slight velvety sheen on an egg's surface.

ELASTOMERIC: A type of flexible or stretchy coating designed to handle substrate movement, bridge cracks and prevent moisture penetration in exterior masonry surfaces, such as concrete and stucco.

ELECTROSTATIC COATING: A coating that's applied by using a spray gun to create an electrical charge on powder particles, while the substrate to be coated is grounded (made neutral); the purpose is to deliver a more efficient, uniform and even coating especially on non-flat surfaces.

EMULSION PAINT: A coating in which the binder is emulsified, and the dominant liquid phase is water; often referred to as latex paint.

ENAMEL: A broad classification of paints considered to be high-quality, hard-surfaced and high-sheen.

EPOXY: A thick, clear plastic-like coating that's used to protect demanding surfaces, such as cement floors, because of its excellent adhesion, durability, and abrasion-, chemical-, corrosion- and water-resistant qualities.

EROSION: The wearing away of a paint film caused by exposure to the elements.

ETCH: The process of wearing away or cleaning a surface, such as bare concrete, with abrasion or corrosion (acid) to increase porosity, and paint or sealant adhesion.

EXTENDER: A cost-reducing additive in paint that has no effect on the color, but provides bulk, extends pigment capabilities and improves other properties. See Filler.

FEATHER SANDING: Tapering the edge of dried paint film with sandpaper.

FERROUS METAL: Metal that contains iron and requires high amounts of carbon content when creating it, generally making it vulnerable to rust when exposed to moisture.

FERRULE: The metal band that connects the handle and the bristles of a paintbrush.

FILLER: A heavily bodied substance used to fill cracks, holes, pores and depressions in a substrate before painting or varnishing; also, cost-reducing extender minerals that improve the efficiency of pigments and add volume to paint. See Extender.

FILLER STRIP: A piece of fluted or beaded wood or plastic that's used to cover an opening in wood, such as a gap between cabinets, or a wall and a cabinet's edge.

FILM: The result of the water or solvents evaporating from paint, and the joining of the binder particles to form a solid protective layer.

FINISH: The last coat of paint or other final coating.

FIRE-RESISTANT: The ability or property of a coating to withstand fire.

FIRE-RETARDANT: The property of a coating to reduce flame spread, resist ignition when exposed to high temperature and insulate or delay damage to the substrate.

FLAKING: The lifting of paint in the form of flakes from the underlying surface.

FLASH: Uneven gloss or color in a dry painted surface usually resulting from irregular paint absorption, insufficiently sealed substrates or poor drying conditions.

FLASH POINT: The temperature at which a coating or solvent will ignite.

FLAT: A non-reflective, no-gloss porous finish. See Matte.

FLAT APPLICATOR: A rectangular, spongy, flat pad with an attached handle that's used to paint shingles and other special surfaces.

FLEXIBILITY: The ability of a coating to expand and contract during temperature changes.

FLOATING: A coating failure that's caused when pigment colors separate on wet paint's surface.

FLOW: The ability of a coating to spread out into a level, smooth film without exhibiting brush or roller marks.

FOG COAT: A pigmented, bonding cement used to coat exterior stucco.

FORCED DRY: Any method that uses heat or air to quicken the drying of a coating.

GALVANIZED: A thin coating of zinc that covers iron or steel to prevent rust.

GLAZE: A thin topcoat from clear to opaque that's applied after the sealer coat, and can change the chroma, value, hue and even out light or dark areas on stained surfaces.

GLAZING COMPOUND: A putty or pliable sealant used to set glass in window frames, and fill nail holes and cracks.

GLOSS: The degree of light reflectivity or shininess of a coating. See Sheen.

GLOSS METER: An instrument that uses a standard scale for measuring the shininess or light reflectance of a paint's surface at one or more angles.

GRAINING: Simulating the grain of wood by means of specially prepared colors or stains and the use of graining tools or special brushing techniques.

GROUND COAT: The base or primary coat of paint; in graining it's often designed to be seen through the topcoat or glaze coat. See Prime Coat and Undercoat.

HARDNESS: The ability of a paint film to resist denting, scratching or marring.

HIDING POWER: The degree to which a paint can hide the previous surface or color.

HOLDOUT: The ability of an undercoat to stop or greatly reduce the topcoat from permeating it.

HOLIDAYS: An application defect whereby small areas are left uncoated or voids appear in the dried paint film.

HOT SPOTS: Green patches of concentrated lime or alkali on plaster, or questionably cured areas on surfaces that paint can't adhere to without pretreatment.

HUE: Any color on the color wheel; different hues are caused by different wavelengths of light.

INHIBITOR: A chemical substance in a coating that slows down or prevents a particular chemical reaction or other process; alters the coating's properties to reduce or resist corrosion, mildew or other undesirable environmental effects.

IN-PLACE MANAGEMENT: The use of maintenance or controls to prevent lead-based substances from becoming exposure hazards.

INTERMEDIATE COAT: The coating between the primer and finish. See Barrier Coat.

INTUMESCENT PAINT: A coating that upon exposure to high heat swells and forms a foam-like, insulating layer over substrates, sealing gaps in the event of fire.

JOINT TAPE: Special paper or paper-faced cotton tape used to conceal joints between wallboards and provide a smooth surface for painting.

KALSOMINE: See Calcimine.

LACQUER: A fast-drying, clear or pigmented coating that dries by solvent evaporation and forms a hard, shiny, protective film on various surfaces.

LAP: To lay or place one coat of paint so its edge overlaps the edge of a previous coat, causing an increased thickness where they meet.

LATEX PAINT: A water-based paint with acrylic binders. Also called acrylic paint.

LEVELING: The ability of newly applied paint or varnish to form a smooth even surface free from ripples, pockmarks and brush marks.

LIFTING: The softening and penetration of a previous film by solvents in the topcoat, characterized by raising and wrinkling in the coating.

LIGHTFASTNESS: A property of a pigment or paint that refers to how fade-resistant a coating is when exposed to light.

LINSEED OIL: A drying oil extracted from flaxseed that's used in paint, varnish and lacquer.

MARINE VARNISH: Varnish specially designed for immersion in water and protection against all climates and mildew. See Spar Varnish.

MASKING: The temporary covering of areas not to be painted.

MASTIC: A permanent bonding agent available in thin liquid, thick glue or paste form, and typically applied with a caulking gun; quick working and best for setting tiles and sealing windows, walls, ceilings and other hard, non-porous surfaces.

MATTE: A type of finish that absorbs light so as to be substantially free from gloss or sheen when viewed at any angle. See Flat.

METALLICS: A type of paint in which the pigment is a metal.

MILDEWCIDE: A substance that kills mildew or inhibits its growth.

MINERAL SPIRITS: A volatile, colorless liquid distilled from petroleum that's used as a paint thinner and solvent.

NAP: The material that covers a paint roller, available in varying fiber lengths to accommodate different surfaces.

NON-FERROUS METAL: A metal that has a higher resistance to rust and corrosion, such as aluminum, brass, copper, nickel, tin, lead, gold and silver, and is used for gutters, water pipes, roofing and more.

NONVOLATILE: The portion of dried paint left after the solvent evaporates. See Solids.

OPACITY: The degree to which a color cannot be seen through, or the ability to hide, mask or obscure a surface or previous coating color.

OPAQUE COATING: A coating that blocks light from penetrating and hides the surface or coating underneath.

ORANGE PEEL: A rough paint surface that resembles the skin of an orange and is caused by poor preparation or application.

OXIDATION: The process of oxygen combining with the binders in paint during evaporation. See Air Dry.

PAINT GAUGE: Instrument for measuring the thickness of paint film.

PATCHING PLASTER: A powder that's mixed with water to create a paste-like, quick-drying substance, and generally applied to cracks and holes in interior plaster ceilings and walls.

PEELING: Strips or sections of paint separating from the surface, usually due to moisture and/or inadequate surface preparation.

PIGMENTS: Paint ingredients that give paint its color and hiding power.

PINHOLES: Small holes that appear when incompatible solvents or air bubbles get trapped in the paint film, expand as they dry and then break through the surface.

PLURAL COMPONENT COATINGS: Fast-setting, solvent-free, high-performance coatings that require a mixing of two or more parts before application.

PNEUMATIC SPRAYER: A method of application that breaks up coating into a fine mist, covering more surface, decreasing time and labor, and producing smooth, uniform coats. Also called automatic sprayer.

POLYURETHANE: Plastic resins in liquid form that dry to a clear, glossy film, and provide solvent- and impact-resistant protection and superior adhesion to any previous finish. Also called urethane.

POLYVINYL ACETATE (PVA): A colorless, odorless, water-insoluble resin used in latex paints and adhesives.

POT LIFE: The amount of time during which paint remains useful after its original container has been unsealed or a catalyst or other additive has been incorporated. Also called spreadable or usable life.

PRIME COAT or PRIMER: A preparatory, or first, coating that's applied to surfaces so topcoats adhere better and last longer. Also called primary coat.

PROPELLANT: The gas used to expel materials from aerosol containers.

PUTTY: A material with high plasticity, similar in texture to clay or dough, typically used as a sealant or filler for nail holes, dents and cracks in wood.

RESIN: The waterborne or solvent-based, film-forming element that bonds paint ingredients together and provides adhesion to substrates; waterborne paints most often contain acrylic resins, or binders, whereas solvent-based paint resins are alkyd. See Binder.

ROLLER: A paint application tool with a revolving cylinder covered with lambs-wool, fabric, foamed plastic or other material.

ROPINESS: Describes a coating that doesn't flow evenly or level out onto the surface, leaving heavy brush marks and a stringy look to the film.

RUST-PREVENTATIVE: A property in paints and primers that slows down or prevents corrosion on metal surfaces. See Anti-Corrosive.

SAFETY DATA SHEET (SDS): An information sheet regarding any hazardous substances that comprise one percent or more of a product's total volume, and emergency protocol in the event of fire, explosion, leak or contact; coating manufacturers must provide an SDS with each product to retailers, who make it available for customers.

SAGGING: A drooping of the paint film immediately after application, which is usually caused by an overly thick application or over-thinned paint.

SAND FINISH: Rough finish plaster or paint that has been texturized with sand.

SATIN FINISH: A pearl-like paint finish that reflects more light than matte and less than gloss; the most universal paint sheen.

SCRUBBABILITY: The capacity of a paint film to withstand frequent scrubbing and cleaning with water, soap and other household cleaning agents.

SEALER: A liquid coating that's formulated to protect porous surfaces, such as wood and plaster, and prevent the absorption of paint or varnish.

SEEDS: Small, undesirable particles or granules in paint, varnish or lacquer.

SELF-CLEANING: Refers to dirt- and water-repellent properties in coatings and adhesives.

SEMI-GLOSS: A radiant coating sheen that reflects light directly.

SEMI-TRANSPARENT: A degree of hiding that falls between translucent and opaque; an obscured visibility.

SET UP: When a coating dries to the point that it's no longer workable.

SHADE: A color made by adding black, which is often more intense and darker than the original.

SHAKE PAINTER: A rectangular-shaped flat pad with an attached handle that's used to paint shingles, shakes and other special surfaces.

SHEEN: Refers to paint's degree of reflectivity. See Gloss.

SHELLAC: Used primarily as a primer or sealer on indoor surfaces since it softens in sunlight; the coating blocks stains, oils, water and odors, such as smoke and urine, from penetrating, and ensures adhesion between coats.

SILICONE: A key ingredient in some caulks and sealants, and characterized by its durability and resistance to chemicals, heat and water.

SKIN: The tough covering that forms on a paint's surface when the can isn't adequately resealed or has been stored in hot temperatures; skinning is when a temperature difference between the can's lid and its contents causes both evaporation of the paint on the lid and condensation on the surface of the paint.

SOLIDS: The part of the coating that remains on a surface after the vehicle has evaporated; the dried paint film. See Nonvolatile.

SOLVENT: The volatile, or liquid, component of coatings that evaporates during drying; any liquid which can dissolve a resin. See Volatile Organic Compounds.

SPACKLING COMPOUND: A thick, paste material used before painting to fill surface defects, such as small cracks, hammer marks, holes and depressions, in various interior and exterior substrates during preparation for painting.

SPAR VARNISH: A glossy, weather-resistant, UV-absorbing varnish designed for use on exterior wood surfaces. See Marine Varnish.

SPECULAR GLOSS: A mirror-like finish.

SPOT PRIMING: Applying primer only to areas that require additional protection, such as stains and rust, instead of the entire surface.

SPREAD RATE: The volume of a coating that can cover a given area, usually expressed as square feet per gallon; it varies with the application method and technique, substrate porosity and the properties of the paint.

STAIN: A partly transparent coating that colors wood without obscuring the grain and/or the texture; also refers to materials that soil the surfaces of coatings.

STIPPLING: A painting technique that requires the pounding of a flat, stiff-bristled brush against a freshly glazed surface to soften brush marks, temper a large expanse of color, disguise imperfections on rough walls or produce a suede-like texture.

STRIP: The complete removal of old finishes or wall coverings with paint removers, sand paper, heat gun or scraping tools.

SUBSTRATE: A surface to be painted.

SURFACE TENSION: The force that causes molecules at the surface of a liquid to be pushed together and form a layer so it can adhere better to a solid surface.

SURFACTANT: An agent or additive that when added to a liquid, reduces its surface tension, thereby increasing its spreading and wetting properties.

TACKY: A condition of a substance, such as a coating, that's not completely dry and slightly sticky to the touch.

TEXTURE PAINT: An alternative to wallpaper, its heavy consistency and coarse grain are used to disguise uneven or imperfect walls, or create a rough-patterned effect on surfaces.

THIXOTROPY: The property of a material that causes it to change from a thick, jelly-like consistency to a fluid upon brushing, rolling, stirring, shaking or heating.

TINT: A color created when white is added, desaturating the original hue and making it less intense.

TINT BASE: Paint that is intended for colorant to be added; each base contains a different amount of titanium dioxide, the key ingredient for achieving desired color and hiding power in paint.

TITANIUM DIOXIDE: The most widely used, high opacity white pigment in paint; exceptionally efficient in scattering light and hiding power.

TONE: Describes the lightness or darkness of a color, and is changed by adding proportions of black and white, or gray, to the original color, making it appear darker or lighter, and less saturated or intense than the original hue. See Value.

TONER: A clear sealer or topcoat with tint that still allows wood grain to show through; applied like a stain, it repels water, provides added protection from UV damage and enhances durability.

TURPENTINE: Distilled, colorless pine oil that's used as a cleaner, solvent or thinner for alkyd paints and varnishes, and has been virtually replaced by mineral and white spirits. See Solvent.

UNDERCOAT: The layer that provides improved adhesion, hiding power and surface uniformity for a topcoat, especially on bare wood.

URETHANE: A synthetic varnish that is exceptionally hard and wear-resistant. See Polyurethane.

VALUE: A measure of the lightness or darkness of a color. See Tone.

VAPOR: The gaseous form of a solid or liquid substance as it evaporates.

VARNISH: A hard, transparent finish or topcoat that protects wood and other surfaces; different varnishes exist for specific needs.

VARNISH STAIN: A varnish that's colored with less pigmented dye than a true stain and leaves a transparent color on surfaces; it's applied by brush or rag, then the excess is wiped or rubbed off before drying.

VEHICLE: The liquid portion of paint, composed mainly of the solvent and binder, with which paint pigments are mixed and dispersed for application.

VINYL: A synthetic resin that contributes to a coating's durability and moisture resistance, but doesn't contain adhesion properties as strong as other binders; better quality paints have more acrylic than vinyl resins and cost more.

VISCOSITY: The thickness of a coating as it pertains to the speed of flow.

VOLATILE ORGANIC COMPOUNDS (VOCs): Organic chemicals in coatings that emit harmful vapors during evaporation; low-VOC paints are considered "eco-friendly" compared to those with higher VOC content. See Solvent.

VOLATILITY: A measure of how quickly a coating evaporates and forms a vapor at average temperatures.

WATER SPOTTING: A paint failure that appears as spotty changes in the color or gloss of a paint film, and results from condensation on the surface during the cure.

WET EDGE: The boundary of a wet paint area that remains workable and to which further paint can be added without visible lapping.

WITHERING: A loss of gloss caused by varnishing woods without filling pores, using undercoating improperly or applying topcoat before the undercoat has thoroughly dried.

WOOD FILLER: A heavily pigmented, pre-finishing product, available in a liquid or paste compound that's used to fill cracks, holes and pores in open-grain woods.

WRINKLING: The development of ridges and furrows in a paint film due to improperly prepared surfaces, harsh weather or heavy application.

ZINC CHROMATE: An anti-corrosive pigment in primers and coatings for steel and aluminum. Also called zinc yellow.

ZINC OXIDE: A white pigment used in paint to reduce yellowing, increase drying and provide resistance to mildew.

About the Experts

Third generation painters Kirby and Tony Hady started Pacific Western Painting, Inc. (PWP) in 2003. Specializing in commercial and residential projects -- particularly HOAs throughout Southern California -- the family-run company takes an educational approach, offering customers instructional information about painting products that work best for their specific needs. PWP continues to experience tremendous growth. In 2016, it was recognized for the third consecutive year as one of the fastest growing companies on the prestigious Inc. 5000 list, which ranks the nation's most successful private companies by overall revenue growth during a three-year period; PWP also has been the recipient of numerous industry awards and certifications. Besides countless HOA communities, PWP's noteworthy projects also include: Hotel Del Coronado, Omni La Costa Resort and Spa, Genentech Inc., and the iconic Hollywood sign.